I WONDER Why

Caterpillars Eat So Much

and other questions
about life cycles

Belinda
Weber

KINGFISHER
NEW YORK

KINGFISHER
LONDON & NEW YORK

Copyright © Kingfisher 2012
Published in the United States by Kingfisher,
175 Fifth Ave., New York, NY 10010
Kingfisher is an imprint of Macmillan Children's Books,
London.

First published 2006 by Kingfisher
This edition published 2012 by Kingfisher

Distributed in the U.S. and Canada by Macmillan,
175 Fifth Ave., New York, NY 10010

Library of Congress Cataloging-in-Publication data
has been applied for.

ISBN 978-0-7534-6708-4 (HC)
ISBN 978-0-7534-6707-7 (PB)

Kingfisher books are available for special promotions and
premiums. For details contact: Special Markets Department,
Macmillan, 175 Fifth Ave., New York, NY 10010.

For more information, please visit www.kingfisherbooks.com

Printed in China
9 8 7 6 5 4 3 2
2TR/0512/WKT/UG/140MA

Illustrations: Martin Camm 4–5, 8–9, 12–13,
14–15, 20–21, 24–25, 28–29; Michael Langham
Rowe 6–7, 10–11, 16–17, 18–19, 22–23, 26–27,
30–31; Peter Wilks (SGA) all cartoons.

CONTENTS

What is a life cycle?

A life cycle is a series of changes that happens to every living thing. It starts from the moment an egg is fertilized and goes on until death. Not all life cycles are the same, but they often follow the same sort of pattern.

Most female insects lay between 100 and 200 eggs in their lifetime, but queen termites can lay up to 30,000 eggs in a single day. Eggs-traordinary!

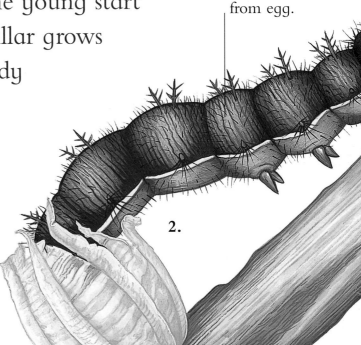

Egg is laid by butterfly.

1.

What is the first step in a life cycle?

The first step in a life cycle is usually when an egg is fertilized. Two adults of the same species (kind) mate and produce young. In butterflies, the young start out as tiny eggs. A caterpillar grows inside each egg until it is ready to hatch.

Caterpillar hatches from egg.

2.

The caterpillar of the monarch butterfly eats a plant called milkweed. If it eats enough, it can get about 2,000 times heavier in just two weeks!

Why do caterpillars eat so much?

When a caterpillar hatches, it eats leaves until it is as big as it can grow. Then it makes a hard case, or pupa, around its body. The caterpillar changes into a butterfly inside this case.

Each life cycle ends when the adult creature dies. But if the creature leaves behind young, a new cycle of life begins.

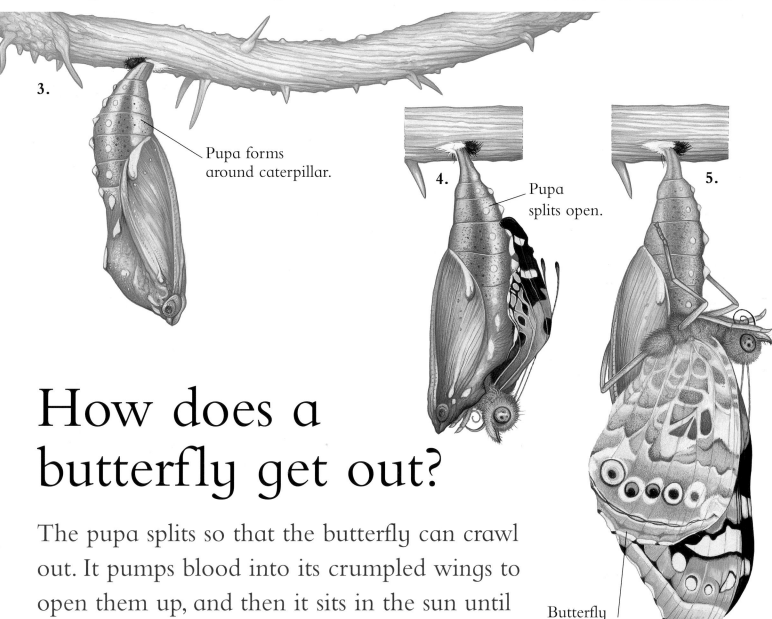

3.

Pupa forms around caterpillar.

4.

Pupa splits open.

5.

Butterfly emerges from pupa.

How does a butterfly get out?

The pupa splits so that the butterfly can crawl out. It pumps blood into its crumpled wings to open them up, and then it sits in the sun until they are dry. The adult butterfly then flies away to find a mate and start a new life cycle.

Do all living things reproduce?

Yes, living things have young to make sure that their species survives. A female pig can have up to 12 babies at a time. When the piglets have grown into adults, they will have babies of their own.

Bacteria can split apart and make millions of young in just a few hours. Some bacteria are harmless, but others can cause infections in people.

Why do animals have two parents?

Most animals, including mammals and birds, have two parents—a male and a female. When they breed, they pass on chemical instructions called genes. Genes control the way a new animal looks and the way its body works.

Mayflies live life in the fast lane! Some live for just a few hours as an adult and must find a mate before they die.

Which living thing splits in two?

Amoebas are shapeless blobs that live in water. They are tiny living things that are made up of only one cell (cells are the building blocks that make up every living thing). Like bacteria, amoebas reproduce by splitting themselves in two.

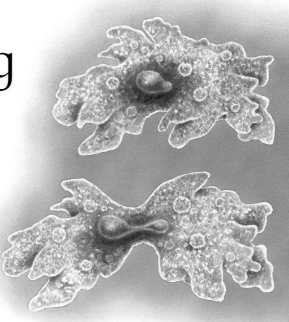

Amoeba splitting in two

Mice and other rodents breed very quickly. A pair of house mice can produce 14 litters, or sets of babies, in just one year!

Why do turtles have lots of babies?

Some animals have lots of babies to make sure that at least some survive. Hundreds of baby turtles hatch at the same time and head for the ocean. Gulls and lizards eat some of them, but because there are so many turtles, a large number will survive.

When a mother shrew moves, her babies form a long line by holding on to one another's tails with their teeth!

Do any animals have just one baby?

Yes, orangutans have one baby at a time. This gives the mother more time to feed and take care of the baby and keep it safe. The baby grows slowly but learns how to survive. This increases its chances of becoming an adult.

Lizard

Gull

Hatching turtle

Do moms and dads get help?

Sometimes, yes. Bee-eaters are birds that eat bees and other insects. Bee-eater parents can't carry enough food to feed all of their babies, so their older children help them out.

Humans usually give birth to one child at a time, but sometimes more. Very rarely, a woman gives birth to seven or even eight babies at once!

Bee-eaters

Do plants have babies?

Most plants produce seeds that grow into new plants. Flowering plants produce seeds when they are fertilized. Insects such as bees help fertilize plants by carrying pollen from one flower to another. A fertilized plant then produces its seeds.

Seeds may be small, but they contain all of the building blocks that a plant needs to grow. A tiny acorn can grow into an oak tree more than 130 feet (40m) tall!

Bees like to eat the dustlike pollen made by flowers. As a bee flies around, it spreads pollen from flower to flower and fertilizes the plants.

Pollen

Foxglove flower (cut open)

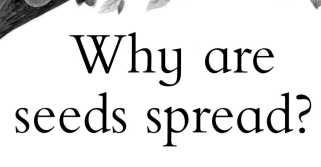

Why are seeds spread?

Seeds need to be spread away from a plant so that they have space to grow. When an animal eats fruit, the tough seeds pass out of the animal in its droppings. The droppings help the seeds grow into new plants.

Fruit-eating monkey

Some seeds have spiky or sticky cases. These get stuck in an animal's fur and are carried to new places when the animal moves around.

Which plant "runs"?

Some plants can make new plants by sending out shoots. Strawberries, for example, produce shoots called runners without being fertilized. They also make flowers that are fertilized and form seeds.

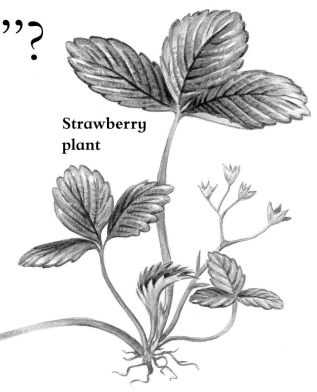

Strawberry plant

Runner

Ladybug larva

Adult ladybug

Hatching egg

Eggs

Do animals make seeds?

No, animals make babies. Not all babies look like their parents. Baby insects, such as ladybug larvae (developing young), often look completely different from adult ladybugs. But as they grow, they change. In time, they will mate and have babies of their own.

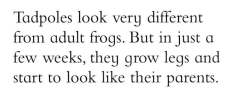

Tadpoles look very different from adult frogs. But in just a few weeks, they grow legs and start to look like their parents.

Why do birds sit on their eggs?

All birds lay eggs, and most of them sit on them until they hatch. They do this because baby birds need warmth to grow. The mother is often in charge of this task, although sometimes the parents take turns.

Egg

**Underground nest
of female platypus**

Do any mammals lay eggs?

Most mammals give birth to live young, but the duck-billed platypus lays eggs. The female platypus lays two or three small eggs. The eggs hatch after about ten days. The mother feeds the babies milk for up to five months.

The platypus is a master builder. It digs tunnels in riverbanks to make safe nests. The entrances to the tunnels are often underwater.

The ostrich lays the heaviest egg of any bird. Each one can weigh up to 3 pounds (1.3 kg)—that's more than a bag of sugar!

Which animal likes snorkeling?

Mosquitoes lay their eggs in still water. When the young hatch, they need to breathe air, so they poke a special tube through the surface of the water. This acts like a snorkel and lets them suck in air.

Some types of woodboring beetle larvae take 40 years to develop from egg to adult!

Breathing tube

Mosquito larva underwater

Emerging cicada

Old skin

How long does a cicada stay young?

A young cicada spends most of its life underground, feeding on plant sap (juice). It stays like this for up to 17 years. It then crawls up a tree, sheds its skin one last time, and becomes an adult. The adult cicada lives for just a few weeks.

Why does a glowworm glow?

The glowworm is a beetle that makes a light in its body. The female has a special organ in her abdomen (lower body) that gives off light. The beetle glows to signal to a male that she is nearby and ready to mate.

Unlike most insects, female earwigs guard their eggs from predators until they hatch.

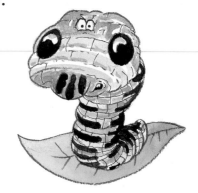

If you threaten an elephant hawkmoth caterpillar, it will suck in air and blow up its head to make itself look too big to eat!

Why do insects hide eggs?

Insects hide their eggs to keep other animals from eating them. Cabbage white butterflies lay their eggs on the undersides of cabbage leaves. This hides the eggs and will also provide fresh leaves for the young to eat.

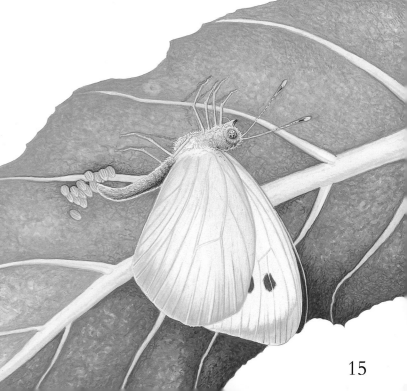

What do spiders keep in sacs?

Many spiders wrap their eggs in a silk sac and carry it around to keep it safe. Green lynx spiders tie their egg sac to a cactus leaf with long strings of silk.

Some spiders cover their egg sacs with mud or dried plants. This disguises them from hungry predators.

What do baby spiders look like?

Baby spiders, or spiderlings, look like tiny adult spiders. Some species of garden spiders stay together for a few days after hatching. They form a tightly packed ball. If they are threatened, the ball splits open and the spiderlings run away.

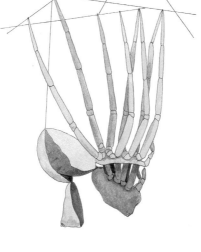

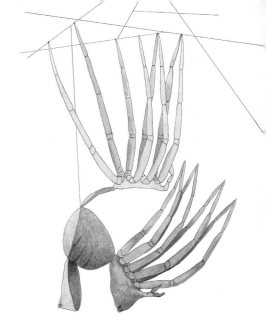

Why do spiders split open?

Like all invertebrates (animals without a backbone), spiders have a tough case around their body, like a suit of armor. When a spider grows, the case splits open and the spider crawls out—bigger. Its skin takes a few hours to harden up.

The female garden spider lays her eggs very quickly. She can lay more than 1,000 eggs in under ten minutes.

Why do spiders go balloooning?

Wolf spiderlings hitch a ride on their mother's back. All of the babies trail silk threads. If they fall off, they climb back up along their thread.

Many spiders are so tiny that they cannot travel far on their legs. But they can hitch a ride on the wind. They spin threads and dangle from them in the air. This is called ballooning.

Do fish lay eggs?

Yes, most fish lay thousands and thousands of eggs. They have to lay so many because only very few will survive to become adults and find their own mates. The female lays her eggs in the water and the male fertilizes them.

Whale sharks are the world's biggest fish, but they eat only tiny creatures called plankton. They slurp up millions in each mouthful.

Male porcupine fish

Eggs

Female porcupine fish

Which fish swallows its babies?

Mouthbreeders, such as cichlids, carry their eggs in their mouths. Even after they hatch, an adult will scoop the little fish back into the safety of its mouth at the first sign of danger.

Male damselfish protect their territory during the mating season and will fight off anything that comes too close— even human divers!

Why do fish dance?

Some fish dance or change color to attract a mate. Male sticklebacks become more colorful when they are ready to breed. They build a nest in the weeds and tempt a female to lay her eggs in it by doing a special zigzag dance.

Male stickleback

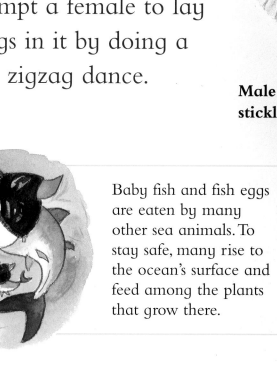

Baby fish and fish eggs are eaten by many other sea animals. To stay safe, many rise to the ocean's surface and feed among the plants that grow there.

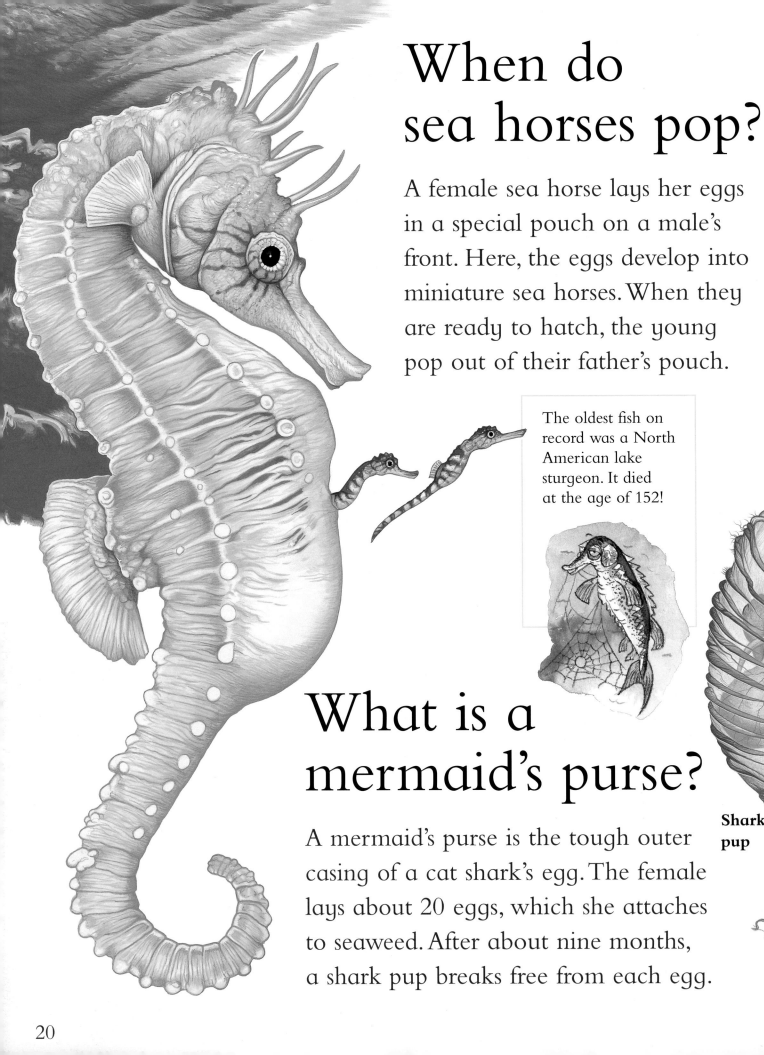

When do sea horses pop?

A female sea horse lays her eggs in a special pouch on a male's front. Here, the eggs develop into miniature sea horses. When they are ready to hatch, the young pop out of their father's pouch.

The oldest fish on record was a North American lake sturgeon. It died at the age of 152!

What is a mermaid's purse?

Shark pup

A mermaid's purse is the tough outer casing of a cat shark's egg. The female lays about 20 eggs, which she attaches to seaweed. After about nine months, a shark pup breaks free from each egg.

Do all sharks lay eggs?

No, thresher sharks give birth to about four live young at a time. A female keeps the eggs inside her until they hatch. The first ones out of the eggs often eat their brothers and sisters.

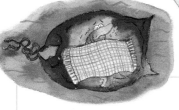

In warm waters, swell-shark eggs develop in about seven months. In colder waters, it can take ten months.

Baby thresher shark being born

Where do baby sharks live?

Lemon sharks are born in shallow lagoons. They are under threat from larger predators when they are babies, but in the lagoons, they live safely, teaming up with other young of about the same size. They stay in the lagoons for about seven or eight years.

Which eggs wobble?

Frogs lay thousands of jellylike eggs that stick together to form a huge wobbly mass. The eggs are called frog spawn. A tiny baby frog, called a tadpole, develops inside each egg. Toads also lay eggs. Their eggs form a long, sticky string up to 3 feet (1m) in length.

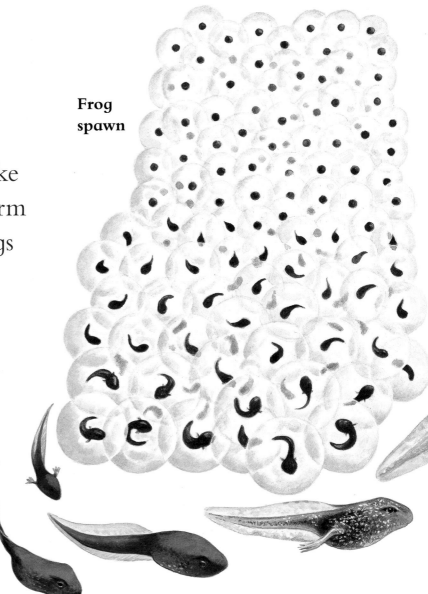

Frog spawn

Red-eyed tree frogs start life with a splash. The female lays her eggs on leaves above pools of water. When the eggs hatch, the tadpoles drop into the pools. They climb back up the trees when they are adults.

How do tadpoles breathe?

When they first hatch from their eggs, tadpoles have long tails for swimming and gills to allow them to breathe underwater. Gills are frilly flaps of skin on the sides of their heads. The tadpoles use their gills to take a gas called oxygen from the water.

Froglets

Why do tadpoles grow legs?

As they become older, tadpoles change. After a few weeks, they grow back legs, then front legs. Their tail and gills shrink back into their body and they develop lungs to breathe air. The small froglets are now ready to start life on land.

When a Surinam toad lays her eggs, the male squashes them into the spongy skin on her back.

Mouth-breeding frog tadpoles live in their father's mouth for the first weeks of life. Then he spits them out!

Why are frogs so noisy?

Many frogs and toads make loud calls to attract a mate. American bullfrogs have a special pouch under their chin. They blow this up like a balloon to make their calls very loud. They can be heard more than half a mile (1km) away!

Why do pythons cuddle their eggs?

Most reptiles lay eggs, which they leave to hatch on their own. But some take care of their eggs, keeping them warm and safe from predators. The green tree python coils around her eggs. By keeping the eggs warm, she helps the unborn babies develop more quickly.

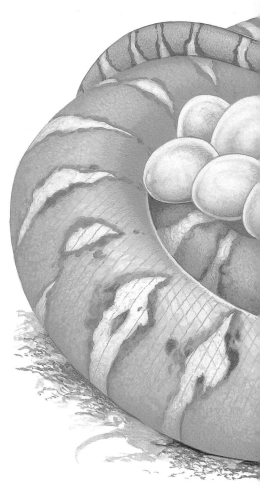

Do crocodiles eat their babies?

A baby crocodile weighs just 9 ounces (250g) when it hatches, but its heavyweight mother weighs 2,000 times as much. Although it looks as if she is eating her babies, she is carefully carrying them from their nest to the water.

Baby rattlesnakes can't make their warning rattle sound. A snake must shed its skin several times before the rattle builds up at the end of its tail.

How do snakes get out of their eggs?

To help them break free of the egg case, baby reptiles have a special egg tooth that slices through the shell. In snakes and lizards, the egg tooth sticks out from the upper lip.

When do eggs yelp?

Crocodiles bury their eggs to keep them warm. But the baby crocodiles cannot dig themselves out. So just before they are ready to hatch, they yelp, grunt, and croak inside the eggs. The mother hears her babies and digs them out of the nest.

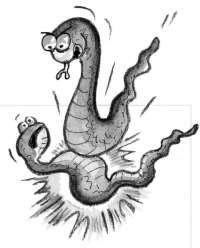

Although male mambas have enough venom (poison) to kill one another, these snakes don't bite when they fight for a female. The males wrestle until the strongest wins.

Why do cranes dance?

Birds find a mate by putting on a courtship display. Male cranes strut around and dance in front of their chosen female, bowing low and then leaping high up into the air.

Hornbills make nests in holes in trees. A female seals herself inside and lays her eggs. Her mate brings her food.

Which bird is a master weaver?

Birds build nests to provide a safe home for their young. The male weaverbird of Africa weaves grasses into a ball-shaped nest that hangs from a tree. If a female likes the nest, she will mate with the male.

Male bowerbirds decorate their nests with bright, shiny things to attract a female!

How do penguin eggs stay warm?

Emperor penguins breed in the frozen lands of Antarctica. The males carry the egg on their feet to keep it warm. They have a special fold of skin under their bellies that helps keep the egg or chick warm.

Who takes care of baby birds?

Cuckoos are such lazy parents! They lay their eggs in other birds' nests. The young cuckoo kills any other chicks that hatch and demands all the food for itself.

Usually, both parents bring food to their chicks. Wandering albatross lay just one large egg that takes about 80 days to hatch. Albatross eat fish, and the parents take turns looking after the egg and going hunting far out at sea.

Which newborn babies can run fast?

Foals (baby horses) can stand up about ten minutes after being born. They can run fast in just a few hours. Like most mammals, foals grow inside their mother for a long time, so they are well developed when they are born.

Female pigs have 12 teats for feeding milk to their young. They can feed a dozen piglets in one sitting!

Why do kangaroos have pouches?

Kangaroos give birth when their babies are still very underdeveloped. A tiny baby is only as long as your thumb. It crawls into its mother's pouch for warmth, safety, and food. The mother produces milk there to feed her baby.

Are tigers good dads?

Male tigers are solitary animals, which means they like to live alone. They never see or care for their cubs. They meet females only when they want to mate.

Whale nudging her baby to the surface

Are any mammals born underwater?

Whales and dolphins give birth to their young in the ocean. Because they are mammals, they need to breathe air, so a mother or her sisters gently nudge the baby up to the surface of the water for its first breath.

Dayak fruit bats from Borneo are unusual because the males can produce milk. They are the only male mammals that are able to do this.

Why do elephant seals fight?

Male elephant seals fight to show who is the strongest. The male that wins the most fights gets the largest territory and will mate with more females.

Male bighorn sheep crash their horns together to see who is stronger.

What happens to old animals?

Most animals don't get very old in the wild. They may not be strong enough to keep up with the herd or they may be hunted down by predators. When they die, their bodies provide food for other animals, such as jackals.

Jackals

Zebra

Why do animals play?

Baby animals learn by playing. When lion cubs chase their mother's twitching tail, they learn the skills they need to hunt. By creeping through the long grasses, the cubs learn how to stalk prey.

Male rhinos leave smelly piles of dung to show females where they are!

Which animals live the longest?

Humans live the longest of all mammals because we have better access to food, water, and shelter than other mammals. In the United States and Europe, men generally live to about 75 and women to 80. But the oldest animal of all time was not a mammal but a 188-year-old tortoise!

Index